WHEN WE ALMOST DROWNED

poems by

Jessica Barksdale

Finishing Line Press
Georgetown, Kentucky

WHEN WE ALMOST DROWNED

Copyright © 2019 by Jessica Barksdale
ISBN 978-1-63534-855-2 First Edition
All rights reserved under International and Pan-American Copyright Conventions.
No part of this book may be reproduced in any manner whatsoever without written permission from the publisher, except in the case of brief quotations embodied in critical articles and reviews.

ACKNOWLEDGMENTS

These poems were first published in the following journals:
Solstice in *The Salt Hill Journal*
When We Almost Drowned, *Revision*, and *But You Put on Your Work Clothes* in the *Suisun Valley Review*.
The Door is a Jar in *Crack*
Conference and *Zaftig Means Juicy* in *Daybreak*
Revision in *Harvest 2001*
Julien at Three in *Rockhurst Review*
If You Are Lucky in *The Peralta Press*
Wondering About Cows in *Gargoyle*
Field of Foals, *Dream of Drowning*, and *Spinning* in *The Smoking Poet*
In a Holding Pattern Over Wisconsin in *Compass Rose*
Pear in *Spittoon*
Crisp in *Diverse Voices Quarterly*
Night Watch in *Straight Forward Poetry*
It's Not Just the Cat and *Automatic Rapture* in *South 85*
Three Witches in *Clare Literary Review*
Gertrude in *The Literary Nest*
Divorce Stats in *The Rain, Party, and Disaster Society*
How to Save Yourself if You're Choking in *The Virginia Normal*
Sugar Bowl in *Lime Hawk*
Privet in *Sheila-Na-Gig*
Bedtime Story in *The Mom Egg*
How to Roast a Pelican in *Crack the Spine*
Before I was a Girl in *Califragile*

Publisher: Leah Maines
Editor: Christen Kincaid
Cover Art: fcscafeine
Author Photo: Rachel Breen
Cover Design: Leah Huete

Printed in the USA on acid-free paper.
Order online: www.finishinglinepress.com
also available on amazon.com

Author inquiries and mail orders:
Finishing Line Press
P. O. Box 1626
Georgetown, Kentucky 40324
U. S. A.

Table of Contents

1.
Field of Foals 1
At the Zebra Crossing 2
Solstice 3
How To Roast a Pelican 4
Sugar Bowl 5
Blood Sugar 7
Before I Was a Girl 9
How To Save Yourself If You're Choking 10
It's Not Just the Cat 12
Dream of Drowning 13
Swim Dad 14
Triggers 15

2.
When We Almost Drowned 19
Crisp 21
Privet 23
Zaftig Means Juicy 24
If You Are Lucky 25
Gertrude 26
The Three Witches 28
Spinning 29
Divorce Stats 30
Morsel 31
So What? 32
Revision 33

3.
Alternate Universe 37
Wondering About Cows 38
Small Blue Basket on Desk 40
But You Put on Your Work Clothes 42
Holding Pattern Over Wisconsin 43
Listen 45
Night Watch 46
Parent-Teacher Conference 48
Bedtime Story 49
The Door is a Jar 51
Julien at Three 54
Rapture 55

1

FIELD OF FOALS

We fed the horse as if playing with fire,
the stolen carrots stuffed into our pockets
and then given to the big black animal
with eyes the color of roasted almonds.
It snorted and snuffed, and though we spoke
a language it didn't, it understood.

One afternoon, the owner
of the Norman farmhouse beckoned,
and we predicted a lecture in French
about responsibility and equine diet.
But the stooped man just waved
us in past the gate, past the front door,
pulling us around the ancient house,
into the pasture, revealing
a field of foals, thin and black and light,
legs like wet sticks. They snuffled up
to our unknown skin, noses pushing
away jacket, coat, scarf, their breath
filled with heat and hay and energy.

I couldn't breathe or speak enough
to ask the right questions, to wonder
how old and which the mare, which the sire.
Instead I reached for my husband
out of habit, grabbed his hand,
both of us exhaling as the foals left us
for the corn bin, both of us
sighing as they galloped off.

We would never return
to feed the horse, to watch the foals,
to have all that life crowding around
our broken marriage. Before we walked
back down the road, we thanked the man
in the language we knew.

AT THE ZEBRA CROSSING

Zebra is a Persian word,
or so the driver tells us as we hurtle
through a bright spring London night
in his C class Mercedes.

In Afghanistan, he tells us,
zebras carefully pick their way
up the craggy mountains, carrying
the Mujhahadeen and their grenades.

He says they wait for daybreak
to attack. When the sun rises,
the men ride the zebras
down the steppes and kill everyone.

The traffic lights turn red, then yellow,
then green. It's London, after all.
Cars drive on the left hand side,
the lights flash in the wrong order,

zebras are from Persia
and carry invaders into the dreams
of sleeping villagers. Not even later,
when I look up the word
can I stop believing
in his story, incorrect,
but true. Everything dangerous
is disguised by something.

SOLSTICE

My brother-in-law carries my dead sister's ashes
to the door. I've been waiting
almost two years, anxious to hold the cheap plastic box,
feel it fit in my hands like an answer.
He doesn't know what to say.
It's one day past the winter solstice, the four o'clock
sun like soot as he leans against
skeleton bones of wisteria.
The woman he will marry in April waits, but
she doesn't matter. Nothing matters
except my sister's last breath as I held her
chest between my warm palms, her eyes glazing silver.
I want to welcome him in my house, catch up
on years of life, repeat the litany
of movement before Rebecca died: Where we were,
what she ate, how it felt to hold a dying body.
I want to hold him even as he backs
away to this new woman, the one who will have
the children Rebecca could only imagine and name.

HOW TO ROAST A PELICAN

If you can catch one,
you must first kill it.
You may stop
out of necessity
or belief system.
But if you're hungry,
if you feel the flesh on your teeth,
wring its neck.

Next, pluck.
I can't tell you how.
I know only pull.
Worse verbs follow:
Slit. Empty. Chop.
And nouns:
Head.
Boning knife.
Blood.

It's like Thanksgiving,
your regularly scheduled program:
dead bird flesh on a kitchen counter.
If times are as difficult as they must be,
build a fire. Cook the bird
without burning the skin.
Do not tempt the fire with what is yours,
what you've worked so hard for.
Never mind the bird
and all the time it took to live
into the body you need
to survive.

Watch the fire. See
wing
water
fish.

SUGAR BOWL

Shark cloud,
spine cloud,
waves of vertebrae
and phalanges
and carpals
and metacarpals
float by, fractured
by light and sky,
bones like the one
in my wrist, the one
I broke at eight.

I'd slipped down
the slickery grass
behind the house.
I'd reached out,
tried to catch myself
before I fell to earth.

Saturday morning,
coffee and sugar
and milk on the table
in my mother's wedding
porcelain, my father
sat reading his paper
when I walked in,
cradling my right arm
like a dead cat.

My mother at the sink,
her back to us,
whispered, Please
*take her to the hospital,
please*. My father
stood up and flipped
the kitchen table
with one hand.

The x-ray's mouth
hummed as it ate my arm,
and the hot wet
plaster of the cast
was white and didn't
smell like dead skin,
not yet. Later,
my father said,
*They looked at me
as if I were beating her,*
and I ate soup with my
left hand and thought of
cracked plates, a milk glass
sheared in half, the lonely
top hat of a shattered
sugar bowl, the clouds
floating over me as I lay
broken on the hill.

BLOOD SUGAR

I moved Rebecca into the garage
next to the WD40 and Castrol oil,
then to my new home, and later I brought her
to a performance where I asked
the audience a question.
I held her box in my hands.
"What am I supposed to do
with my sister's ashes?"
It was the final moment
of my piece, and the lights went out.

I finally decided to plant her
under an pear tree.
I was at Home Depot in the late afternoon,
rain brilliant through outdoor halogens,
and I grabbed up a bargain tree,
the roots clumped
and stiff as witch hair.

At home, shoveling up the muddy
square in the middle of my lawn,
I thought of the labels on Red Anjou pears,
Ripe when yields to gentle pressure.
I thought of Rebecca grabbing
the pear tree branch in my parents'
back yard and swinging up and back,
and then up and down, her body thumping
flat on crabgrass and trampled pears.
My father didn't believe me
when I told him she had fallen
and was holding her broken arm
to her body like a torn doll.

My husband poured her ashes
into the hole, and they were so much
whiter than I'd expected,
not gray and full of souvenirs.

I thought I would find a shard
I would remember, something
I would have memorized
from looking at her skin, from watching
her body grow, from tending her.

I would have spotted her femur,
long and lean. Her collar bone,
rounded like a full moon on her shoulder.
The dust was fine and soft, almost pure,
small flakes luminescent in the dull air.
I feel like touching them, I said,
disgusted with my desire to feel her
once again. *Go ahead*, my husband said,
so I swirled my finger through
the dust as if it were sugar.

BEFORE I WAS A GIRL

I was a streak of light,
a whirl
of every single thought
moving a thousand miles an hour.
A car, a jet, a bird.
I was a pair of pants,
a sturdy shoe,
a thick rope,
a plank of smooth wood,
leather gloves, a saddle,
a hammer, a trowel.
I was the sun. An entire town.
I was yes.
I was never no.
I was morning noon night,
flinging through the grassy
world, beaming, whole, a halo
of dragonflies and dirt.

HOW TO SAVE YOURSELF IF YOU'RE CHOKING

Don't go to that party
with the throat-sized grape appetizers,
the tiny wieners wrapped with puff pastry,
the black olives, the cherry tomatoes,
the slippery stuffed mushrooms.

Don't prepare.
Don't put on your new dress,
zipping it up the back,
imagining someone loved working that last half-inch.
Don't brush your hair, stroke on the blush.
Don't pick up that shiny purse and slip
it over your arm.
Don't imagine walking next
to someone new as you head to his car.
Forget the opened door, the kissed cheek,
the hum of air as you sit
alone for those three seconds, shifting
in your seat until you're just right.

Don't go to the restaurant and order the rib-eye steak.
Don't sit next to him with a glass of burgundy.
Maybe it's Cabernet. Who cares?
You've stayed home to watch the show
everyone is talking about.
The barbeque with the dangerous fish?
The overdone chicken thighs with the splintery bones?
Forget about it.
Scrub the toilet that no one but you will ever use.
Mop the floors.
Clean the windows, pane by pane.

Anything round or tubular or thick.
Anything made for the casual one bite.
Anything on a stick.
Anything sticky.
Anything sugary.

Anything raw-meaty.
Anything eaten with friends.
Anything eaten with strangers.
Anything served where there is laughter and joy and hope.
Don't put any of it near your lips.
Keep your lips shut.
Keep your lips at home.

IT'S NOT JUST THE CAT

You find yourself lost in a city block,
the same streets where you ate hamburgers
with your teenaged boys, the greasy taste
still on your tongue, their boy teases,
their young laughter in your ear.

And then you're idling at a stoplight
in another city, in another block,
and you are pushing a second-hand stroller
up toward the grocery store to buy the food
you can barely afford. Then you're speeding

in your 1972 Squareback,
window open, and you're laughing against
the rush of air, your friend speeding alongside
you in her Datsun, both on your way
to the college you will later flunk out of

but now teach at, the same road you drive
now, window closed. Here you are again,
an unhappy, married woman nearing
middle age, staring up at the Eiffel tower,
not wondering how it was constructed,

but how you will leave your marriage.
Now you sit on a bench on the first platform,
a new husband beside you. Not one life
has ended, the circles only growing, concentric,
all of them over, all of them now.

DREAM OF DROWNING

Not knowing what to grab, I grabbed a man
and then another, their bodies
turning to handles on a sinking boat.

Under water, the fish swam by.
My hair a drift of brown in the night sea, the moon
a wavery slash of white on my puckered skin.

Can you imagine how sorry I felt
for myself, drowning by no fault of my own—
not my storm, not my journey, not my idea

this salt and water and wind—
clutching the handles, the wet wood
pulling me under. Even the moon faded.

Remember the Indian wives, stars of flame
flickering on their husbands'
burning bodies, suttees of failure?

Or what about this? Remember the time
when there was no boat, no water,
just you on that shore you cast

away from? Finally, one hand slipped—
oh how I missed the wood against my palm.
And no, but no, not the other, and then

it was gone, too. Did you know
a blue whale's heart is as big as a Volkswagen?
Did you know that it can submerge

for an hour before needing a breath?
The last of my air bubbles burbled past my eyes.
I hung, wide-eyed, miserable,

so alive even as the bottom feeders
nibbled my shins, even as the whole
of the ocean closed over me, dark and full of stories.

SWIM DAD

In the morning, I made his tea,
added milk, woke him at
four forty-five.

As he drove, I stared slit-eyed
into the five o'clock sky,
the land and trees a gray body

on the shell of the horizon.
The interior light of my father's
1963 Volkswagen, broken

and forever on. At practice,
I shivered through pushups
on iced and sticky cement,

then dove and spun in the
water that crackled with lights.
I was never serious

enough, and I could not see then
that my father was serious only
in his intent, not with his anger,

not with my failures. His love
for me was his desire for my perfection,
my long brown arms pronating

into the water, sleek and solid like eels,
gliding and gliding long after my father
was dead and I swam only for myself.

TRIGGERS

Anything with small animals.
Anything with small animals hurt, potentially hurt, once hurt. Dead. Dead small animals. Dogs with three legs. Two legs. No legs. Dogs that were never born.

Movies with families where something goes wrong.
Movies where the daughter and father hug.
Movies where the father dies, the mother treads water, and the children flip out, one by one. Illness, mental and otherwise, ensues. One of the children develops a chronic disease. Dies.

Mention of elephants, sloths, giraffes, wild African dogs, small green frogs with red stripes, rare bugs no one has heard about.

Facebook pages for babies with terrible problems no one can fix. People who are as small as babies with problems no one can fix. Hungry babies. Hungry children. Some hungry adults. Hungry dogs.

Teen novels where the young protagonist is abandoned by her parents. Maybe the parents are dead. Maybe one has just disappeared. The girl must lie, learns to lie, lies all the time. Has empty sex just to get it over with. No resolution in sight.

Any form of art where a pregnant woman drinks. Everything that is unfair. Polyester.

Television shows where someone divorces for no good reason. Marries again badly. Divorces again. Marries again. Child after child is born. One of the parents dies. No one knows where to send the children.

Any place or book or time or location or movie where anyone is abused sexually. The Donner Party. Jail, prison, death camps, internment camps, medieval insane asylums, latrines.

The destruction of any climate—cold or hot. The overuse of any natural resource. Blowing up of mountaintops for coal. Pit mining. Dam building. The raising, killing, and eating of sentient beings, even snails. Even crickets.

Yelling on the radio. On a daytime talk show. Dr. Phil. Phil Donoghue. Jerry Springer. Maury Povich. Oprah. Rush Limbaugh. Bloggers. Blog trolls. Book reviews. Book reviewers.

Dick Cheney with one leg. Dick Cheney with two. Donald Rumsfeld. Donald Trump. Anyone named Donald. Every politician from the 1980s, especially the demented ones. Anything that is happening now.

Dolls with mouths and eyes that move, ventriloquist dummies, clowns, marionettes, Sicilian puppet shows, nutcrackers, The Nutcracker, sugarplum fairies, Halloween costumes in drugstores.

Anyone whose plastic surgery is obvious.

Anything that lives and then dies. Anything in its dead state. Anything while it is alive.

2

WHEN WE ALMOST DROWNED

In the three o'clock afternoon
sun, we jumped
through Mexican waves.

Toward the horizon,
nothing but Pacific
and bands of light arcing
out of the bay like memory.

We held hands at first,
but the ocean was rough, the waves
twisted with salt and recent storm.
So we tread water, the beach
bobbing up and down
in our view.

I don't know at what point we realized
we were in danger, when the water,
unrelenting, hit our heads too often, too quick.
There was a look between us, an idea
that it was time to go to shore now,
one second later would be too late.

Even though we were together,
and I knew he could save us both,
I kicked my legs to the beat of my long ago
swimmer's body, the muscle memory
rekindled by adrenaline.
I pulled after him, breathing toward land.

Now in bed, one of us will say, "Do you remember
when we almost drowned?"
And I am never quite sure
which time we mean, our marriage
stretching fifteen years since Mexico,
pulling us away from land and each other
a hundred times or more.

But the other will nod, silent
for that second, then saying, "Oh, yes."
And maybe, we will touch
because we know we've saved
each other since.
Mexico was only the first time
we had to pull hard, one after the other,
desperate for shore.

CRISP

The cafeteria women
behind the counter
wearing white caps
made an apple crisp
you never forgot.

There you were,
a small, brown boy living
on a brown hill,
this America still new.
In order to think
apple
you had to think
manzana
first.

But this crisp—
cinnamon, butter, brown sugar
and apples cooked soft
and golden—lived in you
long after *manzana*
was the word you
had to dig for.

In the first years of
our marriage, I tried
every recipe, searching
for the exact taste
you craved, stalking
the secret, the way
to get to that part of you.
But nothing came close
to the childhood
crisp, not a brown betty
or kugel or crumble.
Nothing I found
brought back the sweetness

you thought you remembered,
and eventually,
I stopped trying.

PRIVET

You hate the tree the neighbors
allowed to grow wild between the houses.
Thin and spindly—barely a tree at all—it unfurls
its scraggly umbrella to whisk both roofs.
Lazy, deciduous, it drops pollen, leaves,
fat handfuls of black berries,
seedlings sprouting, green terrors
latching into the wet earth, ready to burst
into rows of scraggly hedges.
Your neighbors are bad gardeners;
they water late at night, sprinklers
shuddering, and refuse to share
fence repairs. Your own gardener does not
pay attention to the berry bunches
clumped in the agapanthus, rhododendrons,
persimmon. Every spring morning,
you scurry and sweep, pull and pluck,
cursing under your breath.
Today, through an upstairs window,
a swoosh and flurry. The privet
bends and shivers, heavy with more
than its own dark fruit. On every branch,
a glimmer of soft pale brown, yellow,
slash of black-masked eye, red-tipped wing.
A flock of ravenous cedar waxwings
rock the tree, swaying fat on the treetop,
eating the blessed berries, whirling
with bird joy and ferocity at the sudden
bounty. You crouch at the sill,
hand to mouth, blood whirring
like the birds, who hate
no one, no
thing.

ZAFTIG MEANS JUICY

Ripe and round,
I slip my finger
against the slim
band of my underwear,
slide the skin
of my dress
over my head,
plunge the fruit
of my body into a hot
tub of water that stretches
out toward ocean.
I am Aphrodite
simmering in her shell,
radiant, resplendent,
luscious as a summer plum.

IF YOU ARE LUCKY

You ask yourself
how a fat woman
can be pretty,
even though you are pretty
and you are fat.

At a café, a man
at the next table leans over,
half-whispers,
"I've read that," points at your
book. He smiles, stares
at your lips, and all you
do is nod, silent.
After a minute he sighs, says,
"Well, it was a good try,"
and you wonder
what is wrong with him.

In the mirror
a flap of flesh,
large arms.
You try on a dress
with eyes closed, opening
them as if you expect
an explosion.
But, yes.
It fits.

Some days, if you are lucky,
no mirrors. No memory
of what you saw
yesterday or the day before,
only luxury in your step,
a one-two of hip, your hair
up and down
on your shoulders, breath
in and out, a fire
you feel everywhere.

GERTRUDE

Queen, widow, mother,
new-made wife surprised
by late love, a middle-aged blush
on your still fair cheeks.

The flies in the ointment:
Your disturbed son and the hasty
everything of your first husband's
death and your second marriage.

You don't even know
about the orchard murder
or the nightly ghost.
How you wish

Hamlet would settle down,
so you could be the maid
rushing head first into long nights
of song and feasting.

You want laughter.
You want to believe
that something this good
can last. But that's where

the story always ends,
the truth in the cup
you just sipped from, your eyes
on the man for whom

you gave up everything.
How you can imagine in that last,
strangled moment, the unsipping
of the poisoned wine,

the backing away
from the clanging weapons,

the slipping outside the castle,
the bright afternoon all around you.

THE THREE WITCHES

They were nearing fifty,
three beautiful witches
with dark chocolate
and red wine in the afternoon
living room, talking about
thinning hair, dry skin, a problem
uterus. One described
dousing the scalp
with onion juice. Another said
she would have kept the baby,
though it turned out to be
a fibroid, not a child.
The other talked of olive oil,
applied liberally, everywhere.

Now they are in their late
seventies, at the jumping-off point,
wearing one-piece swimsuits
and thick rubber swim caps,
the three of them at the wag end
of the high dive, bouncing
up and down, up and down,
smiling back at me as I climb
the ladder, waiting for my turn.

SPINNING

In the strange garage of the old French
house, I found a stationary
bicycle, the pedals loose, the seat
a hard plastic wedge.

Every morning I rode, spinning nowhere
as I read novels in a language
I can barely speak.
One the story of a woman

with horrible neighbors. I still don't know
what they did to her. Outside,
August was full of sun
and particulate matter.

My husband would hike in the forest
along the ridge, come home
with tarts, juice, tales of the baker's
daughter with the big smile.

Over coffee, I'd have no stories
he wanted to hear, my thoughts
on home and how once
we got there, I would leave him.

DIVORCE STATS

Agencies contacted, offices visited, emails sent to change name back to maiden: 17
Apologies still owed (mine): 26
Bottles of wine consumed alone: 104
Boyfriends with a hair-pulling problem: 1
Dating sites joined: 3
Difference in age between ex-husband and his new wife (he older): 17
Difference in age between my second husband and me (he older): 7
Debt incurred: 32,000
Husbands: 2
Moves since I left my first husband: 6
Number of years before it seemed reasonable to keep on living: 1.2
Perfect first dates that never turned into second dates: 1
Perfect first date that turned into a marriage: 1
Projected age of baby, the one he pleaded for in those last days: 9.5
Really bad, sometimes scary dates involving toupees, brown teeth, sad lives (mine included): 12
Sons who think parents ended up with better partners: 1
Sons who blamed me for everything: 1
Sons who are okay with the way things are now: 2
Sons: 2
Students who deserve a partial tuition refund (2005-2006) due to insanity, absence, and erratic behavior (mine): 242
Time it took for my mother to forgive me: Unknown
Times my heart broke and broke again: 123
Years since I gazed out at a brilliant fall morning, certain I wasn't going back: 8
Years between date of separation and marriage number two: 5
Years taken off life due to self-pity: 3.2
Years added back to life span due to better circumstances: 3.6
Years it will take before September is only the end of summer, the leaves and earth turning and not because of me: 1. Maybe 2.

MORSEL

You ignored the small ways everything began
to fall down, disintegrating into ashy bits
you prayed were autumn leaves. The marriage
turned at the rolled eyes, year six, you in the back
seat with the second baby, he at the wheel,
"Fucking Magellan" who could find
the freeway, goddammit.
Your friend listened to your dream
about the other man, her eyes wide
and compassionate, her hand reaching out, warm.
The next day she lifted your conjured
infidelity for a poem. How many years
did you abide the swift stealing
of your imagination? And what about this
world, the knocks on doors, the pulling
of fathers from cars, the felling of laws
and rights, the overlords assuming
their ancient places? You shrugged
at the messes the same way you denied
your marriage, and kept calling your friend,
setting a date, picking the restaurant, telling
your stories, amazed each time she stole
the red wine, the man, the Paris street corner,
as if you hadn't handed her every detail, laughing,
digging inside yourself for the last juicy morsel.

SO WHAT?

I'm sick of you already, this poem says,
tired of the stories that go back
half a century, the same small drum
beating on and on and on.
Wait a minute, I begin, but the poem
won't let me write about the doll.
Not again, it groans. So what
if your father made you throw it away.
And please, for the love of all
that is holy, skip the ugly rubber boots
your mother pulled over your shoes
every winter day of kindergarten.
No one wants to hear about it.
What about the yelling, the house
a rage of thrown pots, smashed plates,
flipped tables? The poem shrugs
and turns away. Come back
when you have something original.
You've wrung the sheet
of your woeful first marriage
a few times recently. Your dead sister,
dead father, lost hopes, feelings
of otherness, please. What a damn mess.
Give me a chance, I say, trying
to conjure up a new strain of trauma.
I'm leaving, says the poem.
You aren't being specific or even
interesting. There isn't one simile,
pop culture reference, or literary allusion.
No slice of life that makes mine
feel lived. Stay here holding your doll,
wearing your bad boots.

REVISION

In my dream, I have the chance
to raise my sisters all over again.
They have just been born
but backward, the youngest
a curly-headed toddler;
my middle sister an infant in my arms.

I am intent on doing things right.
I've told my mother that it will
all be different. I imagine
our recreated lives, perfect enough
to keep Rebecca alive.
This time, Sarah will be loved.
In my dream she smiles up at me,
a cuddly, different child.

But then I think, This is not mine
to do better. These are not
my children, and what about me?
Don't I deserve the happiness
I couldn't pull out of the earlier life

But I tie on my hat,
hold the babies next to my body,
and head back to Oklahoma
alone, without my mother,
without my father
who has left us in the dream, too.
I take my siblings back to the place
our family came from long ago,
as if I could write our lives
into an entirely different story.

3

ALTERNATE UNIVERSE

Imagine you learned to not be ashamed,
a feeling poured into your bones instead of marrow.
For the sake of this poem, let's call it age five.
Imagine the first day of school, you leaning
into the small warm bodies of children,
not caring that your mother couldn't dress you.
Imagine you had straight, even bangs.
Maybe you put on the ugly white boots
before she asked, the kind that, instead of being shoes
pulled over shoes, the kind no one wore
in California, the kind you became, something
covering you, but inside you were still there.

Imagine you traveled with your pregnant belly
to another state, a better school, one
that would have made you a better person.
Imagine you didn't crave him,
marriage, the family you'd always wanted,
doing it right, the exact opposite of your parents.
Keep going back, back. Let's imagine
you never slept with him. Yes, I know. The children.
But imagine you don't know about them,
that in this alternate universe, there will be
other children. Imagine you are strong enough
to do it. You know what I'm talking about.
Things aren't working, haven't been working
for years. But look at you, scared, even after all
you survived—the bad jobs, the wrong friends,
the weather of northern cities. Imagine
we pack your bag. Wait, finish this poem,
and imagine this: We stand and walk downstairs.
Grab what you need, which isn't much.
The children are grown and gone. It's summer,
weather big enough to hold possibilities.
You don't need a sweater. Or boots.
Let us get those unruly dogs and hop in the car.
I'll shut the garage door.
You drive.

WONDERING ABOUT COWS

I'm at a beef restaurant,
cow skulls on the walls, rusted
farm implements clanging
against counters. A stiff brown hide
stretches to the door. A hot plate
of deep fried onions glistening
before me, I'm thinking of my sister's
last words: *Leave me alone.*
My grandmother, just last week,
said, *Get me out of here*,
then jerked into a coma.
I'm sitting here wondering
about cows, how they plow
forward with honey eyes, move
toward a blazing iron rod.
Then they are boiled, skinned,
turned into dinners, and guess what?
My New York strip covered
with mushrooms is here, and I think
about my sister, whose body
died slowly, from the inside out,
dead Islets of Langerhans
languishing in her pancreas,
diabetes fitting her like a harness,
existence bit, bones and flesh
and heart and blood losing structure,
eyes turning into the same cow eye
I dissected in high school,
sophomore year. I remember
poking the glimmering sclera,
the clear full underside of vision,
laughing, saying *sclera, sclera*,
for weeks because it was so odd,
so detached, a perfect blob of matter
in a plastic dish. I am cutting
into medium-well flesh, thinking
about my other sister, the pathologist,

and how she slices into bodies
of strangers, how she studies
what goes wrong. She told me—
after we turned off the oxygen
and pulled out the wires and tubes—
our sister's brain was an empty
viscous sphere, and she would know,
her sharp metaled hands cutting
into brains enough, and I wonder
about my grandmother's brain,
deprived of oxygen because
the cancer filled her lungs as air
once had. Two weeks ago, she
ran naked to a friend's apartment,
carrying a silver-wrapped gift,
certain the police were coming
to arrest her. *Hypoxia*, my uncle calls it.
He's a pathologist, too. I have finished
my meal. I sit back, admire the hide view.

SMALL BLUE BASKET ON DESK

A tiny useless screwdriver,
a hair band,
bent paperclips,
random earbuds,
heart-shaped dog tag.
An extra car key,
a sedimentary rock
from Sicily or Scotland.
I can't remember.

FaberCastell® Pink Pearl 100 eraser.
Stiff and pink.
Hard to the touch.
Impossible to bend.
Doesn't remove anything.

Cracked iPod, one I bought for myself.
Inscribed on the back:
Don't steal this.
No one did.
I broke it instead.

First husband's wedding ring.
Gold. We swapped one year, mine
too wide, too big. His just right.
Then I left him.

Dead father's magnifying glass.
Snatched years ago from his desk drawer,
left-hand side, just after he died.
Plastic rim, stitched leather case.
Made in Japan,
just after the war,
everything still occupied.

Unused *Forever* stamp.
The question: Does forever

last forever?
Or: How long
does forever last?

BUT YOU PUT ON YOUR WORK CLOTHES

In late September, the winds
blow down redwood leaves
brittle as brown combs,
clusters of maple seeds
like the dead half wings of butterflies,
wisteria branches broken and cracked
by heavy pods. The air is still
when you leave in the morning,
but hot noon winds
whip up from the Bay,
pull the mountains to the shore,
prune with reckless hands, leaving you
nothing to do but rake up the mess.

When you come home, hours later,
you can't see your geranium or salvia,
everything buried, almost
as if you had never planted a thing.
But you put on your work clothes,
lace your leather boots,
and beat back the heavy air
with an afternoon energy,
just as your heart has learned,
again and again, to push
at the wall of your chest,
to keep you moving
when it would be
easiest to lie down.

HOLDING PATTERN OVER WISCONSIN

In a holding pattern over Wisconsin,
I contemplate my marriage.

Sky swirls past in jagged arcs of white
and black and silver. The flight attendant

passes out bags of non-peanut snacks,
careful lest anyone die from something

other than wind shear or engine malfunction
or terrorist blade. I lean back, knowing

when I land, I will be single again,
living in a cottage I rented weeks ago.

My youngest son shrugged, said the place was nice,
but wondered when the old person smell

would dissipate. I wanted to tell him
soon enough, I would smell that way

myself. All he has to do is wait a little longer,
keep coming to visit, watch me fall apart

and flake like salt into the carpet. The captain
crackles in, tells us all of Wisconsin

is on high alert. I look out the window,
certain I can see thousands of people leaving each

other, wives and husbands packing bags
and moving down the street into cottages

that smell like papery, ancient skin.
Every morning, they pretend they are content,

make dark coffee, read the entire paper

in complete silence. Then one morning,

they no longer pretend. They don't have to.
I can't tell you how this happens.

Finally, they can see something they imagined
they only dreamed. Laughter. A glass of wine.

A nice conversation. I press my nose against
the window, desperate to see these dreams,

hoping that in between waves of flung water,
I'll spot happiness. The captain tells us we might

have to fly to another state altogether, avoiding
the torrent of Wisconsin, the terrible winds,

the freezing rain. I chew my pretzels,
knowing even as I circumnavigate

an angry funnel of water and sky, I'm going
nowhere yet, no matter where I fly.

LISTEN

In a month of divorce and brain tumors and premature babies
and wars in far-off places, you decide to ignore the ugly dream
of the world. In a month of adultery and deceit and bad behavior
(all yours) you decide to love yourself. Yourself as you are.
You realize how ridiculous it is to start now, forty-two,
overweight (slightly), drooping (slowly), even on the outside,
so impossible to love. But it's too late to do anything else.
How long have you listened to the voice in your head?
The one that sounds like your grandmother's pinched
whine about tight blue jeans and messy hair. Or maybe
it's a version of father, mother, husband, teacher, lover, friend.
It's been so long since you've heard your own voice,
you don't remember what you sound like. You pick up
a conch and press it to your ear, the way you pressed a shell
to a child's at a party last week. *What's that?* she said,
her mouth and eyes the shape of the world you want,
round and lovely and open. *Listen*, you said,
hear something new. It's the ocean calling you.

NIGHT WATCH

You pull yourself
from the bottom
of an empty well,
the brick walls slick
and dark with rainwater.

You yank yourself
up for what feels like hours,
your mind a strange
lingering, half dream,
half waking.

You shouldn't be here
now, the house silent,
the outside quiet
of birds, empty
of children's voices.

You need to fall back
down the hard well,
but instead, you slip
out of bed, pad the cool
carpet, remember another

nighttime life,
when the babies awoke
and it was just you
and them in a yellow-lit room,
nothing but their soft,

needy sounds and the hush
of night air.
You're alone now,
the babies grown,
but as you walk upstairs,

you imagine you hear

their cries, feel their warm
bodies against yours.
You remember when
the night needed you.

PARENT-TEACHER CONFERENCE

I have been sent to the office,
again, like before, but now

I am the parent, my son the one
not listening, not doing homework,

picking an attitude from the anguished
teenaged prop room, fumbling

for ideas on how to be a person.
I was often in this small, airless cube,

taking to Miss Giddings about my D's
and F's, my desire to be a stewardess,

as *Seventeen* magazine and romance novels
had taught me, nothing mattered

but flawless skin and love. What can I say
to this counselor, this teacher,

two young women, women like me who
want to teach and pass on the knowledge

they'd learned to take from others. I nod,
wish that life were smooth somehow,

like glass, like the reflection off
a shiny page, like something I once read.

BEDTIME STORY

As I write the words
protest, obstructing, and *battery,*
a slick black raven
flaps to the lowest
limb of the half dead
cypress and begins to
pluck clean a baby robin.

If I weren't on the phone
with a legal aide,
I would be more upset.
I might think *raven murderer*
and then laugh a dark
little laugh, thinking
we need more than one raven
to make a murder.

The aide talks on.
My son has been bused
to Santa Rita jail,
where the real criminals go,
that barbed-wire-protected
concrete block I used to pass
in my 1968 Volkswagen
on my way to teach English,
my two little boys
and first husband back home
reading bedtime stories.

The raven one, two, three
stabs the limp body,
feathers flying.
Even behind the window glass,
I hear the *bop bop bop*
of his hard bill as he hits
branch through flesh.
My son is in a big box jail,

visitors from eight till noon.
I write *lawyer, Tuesday,
arraignment.*

If I were outside, I'd yell
until the raven flew off.
I'd sweep the feathers
from the patio. But no
matter what, the chick
would still be dead.

THE DOOR IS A JAR

The door, the dark wood,
is a jar with a view.

When the stories flash
open, I kick them wide,

hold them panoramic until
a hand reaches in, pulls out

a scene—perhaps an infidelity,
a man in a T-shirt stained

with coffee and her smells,
haggard eye, bed-messed hair.

He is watching the window,
elbows on knees, thinking

of the perfect lie to tell his wife.
The woman, no clothes, one

breast in bra cup, the other
adamant, angry. She has waited

in hallways, eager for his voice,
walking softly in high heels

to catch him as he leaves
the elevator, worn her best silk

blouse every week, a button open,
freshwater pearls above her breasts

like stars. He sighs, and her fist grips
a red lipstick, points toward the man,

whispering, You never loved me,

did you? I breathe in the air, taste it,

rub it on my face, spread it on this page.
A young girl on a yellow bus,

chin resting on a rattling sill.
She sees the car of a neighbor boy,

cross-eyed headlights wrapped
around a utility pole, bystanders,

police at the corner, the side view
of a woman—the boy's mother,

she's sure—walking from the scene
wearing a white knit hat, her right eye

open, her thin fingers cupping her nose
so carefully , and when the girl arrives

at school, she sees the boy, hears
what the other children are whispering.

Seconds later, the boy is pulled from class.
Just before summer, his father moves

across town, marries another woman,
the girl doesn't see the boy until high school

when she finally understands
the woman walking away was crying.

I let the door go, it closes, and my eyes
and face are a flesh slash against wood.

A girl in a hospital room has a drug dream
of her dead grandfather sitting by her bed,

offering her the sour cherry candies
he kept in his doctor's office. She sucks them,

looks at his brown face, smells Florida,
wet fishing line, a dangling grouper,

flounder, grunt. She feels small stabs
on her thighs, bites down on the candy,

touches bandages on her legs, thinks about
burns, thinks about sections of skin

stripped off her belly, placed on her shins
like gum. She gets off the bed, firecrackers

exploding on her legs, the band playing
for America, and she runs down

the hospital corridor, looking for her
grandfather, or her mother, someone

to tell her what to do with her legs,
to show her how to lift the line,

grab the enormous fish. The light,
the woman with the man, the boy

without a mother, the girl with a dream.
I palm the knob, shut it tight.

JULIEN AT THREE

When you heard the jangle
of my particular key chain,
you kicked through playground
tan bark, jump-landed
on hot asphalt, your elbows
swinging, your hair curled wild
as you swung your head
side-to-side, your denim jacket
flying behind you like a magic cape.

No one ever came to me like that,
wanted me that much, pounding
into my arms, your dirt-soap-boy
smell, your clothes streaked
with paint, crayon, glue, your knees
rough and ashy from hours
of outside play.

You pressed your wet open mouth,
tangy with afternoon fruit snacks,
on my own, and I could understand
how monsters ate their young, gobbled
down all the goodness because
it was almost unbearable to watch
such amazing beauty in the world,
in my arms, your wet sand skin
on my shoulder, your black eyes
full of my reflection, your sticky fingers
in my hair, pulling me, pulling me
into the moment so I'd know
it would end.

RAPTURE

I want it to be quick
and sharp like a vaccine
or a crackling slap in the face.
I want it to shoot me up
before I have the time to say
goodbye or sign my will.

I want it to be more
exciting than clouds and harps.
More space shuttle, less
St. Peter. I don't want
a body or skin or shape.
I want to be bigger

and less than, able to cover
everything or slip through
the eye of god's needle,
if god is there at all,
much less sewing. I want
to recline on the beach

of a new moon and think
about nothing, and then
I want to disappear into
the atoms I once was, all of this
happening so fast, I think
I'm still here typing.

Additional Acknowledgments

It is impossible to acknowledge all the people who helped me with these poems over the years. So I thank you all, teachers, editors, publishers, and readers, but most specifically: Kris, Julie, Marcia, Judy, Gail, Keri, Joan, Maureen, Jackie, Ía, Susan, Marj, Darien, and Warren, my true writing confidants and guides.

And love and thanks to those who have given me everything to write about: Michael, Mitchell, Julien, Carole, Jesse, Rebecca, Sarah, Mitch, Vida, and Val.

Jessica Barksdale's fourteenth novel, *The Burning Hour*, was published by Urban Farmhouse Press in April 2016. A Pushcart Prize and Best-of-the-Net nominee, her short stories, poems, and essays have appeared in or are forthcoming in the *Waccamaw Journal, Salt Hill Journal, Little Patuxent Review,* and *So to Speak.* She is a Professor of English at Diablo Valley College in Pleasant Hill, California and teaches novel writing online for UCLA Extension and in the online MFA program for Southern New Hampshire University. She holds an MA in English Literature from San Francisco State University and an MFA from the Rainier Writers Workshop at Pacific Lutheran University.